YOU HAVE EVERYTHING YOU NEED.
IT'S HERE, IN YOU, ALWAYS.

---

fight on

COMPENDIUM®
live inspired.

WRITTEN BY **M.H. CLARK** ~ DESIGNED BY **SARAH FORSTER**

IF YOU LOOK CLOSELY, CAREFULLY, PAST THE CHALLENGES, THE TURNS IN THE ROAD, AND ALL THE DISTRACTIONS, YOU'LL NOTICE SOMETHING: **YOU ARE DOING IT.**

RIGHT NOW, YOU ARE DOING IT. DESPITE ALL THE BACKGROUND NOISE, AND THE CHALLENGES, AND THE DISTRACTIONS, AND THE DOUBTS THAT TELL YOU OTHERWISE, YOU ARE DOING IT. YOU ARE CREATING YOUR BEAUTIFUL LIFE. YOU ARE TRAVELING IN THE RIGHT DIRECTION.

SET ASIDE YOUR DOUBTS. QUIET THE THOUGHTS THAT SAY YOU AREN'T GOOD ENOUGH, IMPORTANT ENOUGH, CAPABLE ENOUGH TO BEGIN. TELL THEM YOU CAN'T LISTEN BECAUSE TODAY YOU TRUST YOURSELF. TODAY, YOU BELIEVE IN YOUR HEART. TODAY, YOU TELL THE SMALL VOICE INSIDE YOU'RE GIVING IT A CHANCE.

TODAY, BE BOLD. BE STRONG.

fight on

YOU
ARE *NOT*
HERE TO
IMITATE.

You are not here to follow along.

YOU ARE HERE

TO DELIGHT IN

YOUR POTENTIAL.

YOU ARE HERE

TO DO THE

THINGS THAT

ONLY YOU CAN DO.

YOU ARE ALLOWED TO SAY NO.

YOU ARE ALLOWED TO LET GO.

YOU ARE ALLOWED TO PROTECT YOURSELF.

YOU ARE ALLOWED TO ENJOY YOURSELF.

YOU ARE ALLOWED TO PUT YOURSELF FIRST.

If you knew how capable you are, you'd stop worrying and start amazing yourself.

LISTEN TO
THE KIND,
WISE, AND
KNOWING
THINGS
PEOPLE SAY
ABOUT YOU.

BELIEVE THEM.

BE COURAGEOUS.

The person you have been
is not the person
you will remain.

Think of this
as both a challenge
and a gift.

YOU WERE MADE FOR SOMETHING SPECIAL.

BE PATIENT.

The world is arranging itself.

YOU DO NOT HAVE TO
SEE THE WHOLE PICTURE
BEFORE YOU KNOW IT
IS **BEAUTIFUL**.

YOU DO NOT HAVE TO
UNDERSTAND IT ALL TO
MOVE FORWARD **IN FAITH**.

YOU DO NOT HAVE TO
KNOW THE ENDING IN
ORDER **TO BEGIN**.

DO NOT

GIVE YOUR TIME TO THE THINGS THAT DRAIN YOU, THE THOUGHTS THAT BRING YOU DOWN, OR THE PEOPLE WHO BREAK YOUR HEART.

MAKE ROOM

FOR GOOD THINGS

TO BEGIN.

TAKE A CHANCE.

fight on

You are not required to change all at once. You are required to be brave enough to make small changes one day at a time.

YOU ARE ALREADY ENOUGH.

THERE IS NO ONE IN THIS WHOLE WORLD YOU'D

CRITICIZE THE WAY YOU CRITICIZE YOURSELF.

START FORGIVING MORE.

Start with you.

Just because your miracle doesn't look like the miracle you were expecting, that doesn't mean it isn't the one you've been waiting for.

TAKE A RISK.

YOU DO NOT NEED ANYONE TO **LIGHT UP YOUR LIFE.**

There is great joy in discovering you can do that for yourself.

YOU WILL BE PRESENTED
WITH OPPORTUNITIES TO EXCEL,
OPPORTUNITIES TO STRUGGLE,
OPPORTUNITIES TO BE SIGNIFICANT,
OPPORTUNITIES TO BE HUMBLED,
OPPORTUNITIES TO CRY HARD,
TO BE FOOLISH, TO LOVE.

TAKE THEM.

Yes, there is pain.
There is beauty too.

KEEP YOUR
HEART
Open.

THERE WILL BE TIMES
WHEN YOU FIND YOURSELF
RIGHT IN THE MIDDLE
OF THE PLACE YOU
ARE MEANT TO BE.
INVITE THOSE TIMES.
NOTICE THOSE TIMES.

Live for them.

YOU CAN.

LEAVE
ROOM
FOR
DELIGHT.

YOU ALREADY KNOW THE ANSWER.

YOUR HEART AND SOUL
HAVE BEEN TELLING IT
TO YOU ALL ALONG.

THERE IS **NOTHING** WRONG WITH STARTING AGAIN.

MAKE IT
HAPPEN.

TRUST YOURSELF.

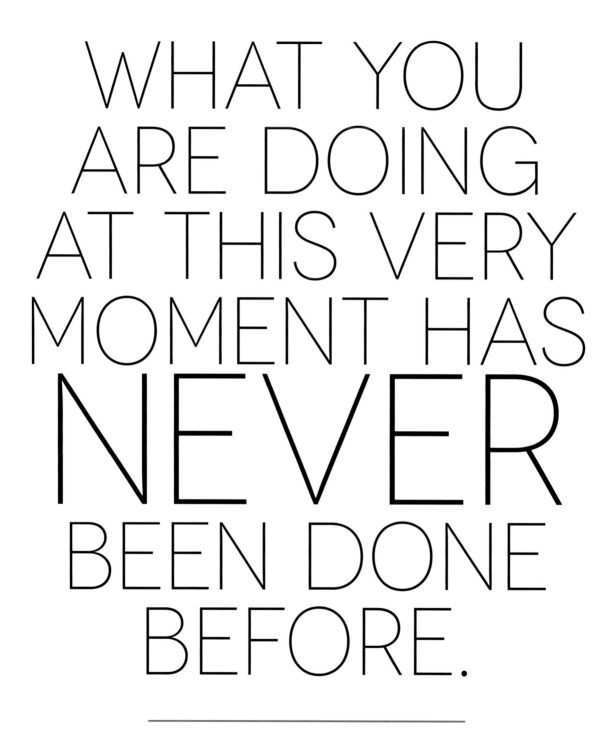

WHAT YOU
ARE DOING
AT THIS VERY
MOMENT HAS
NEVER
BEEN DONE
BEFORE.

DON'T BE AFRAID TO EXPERIMENT.
**DON'T WORRY IF YOU NEED A FEW CHANCES
TO GET IT RIGHT.**

LIVE THIS
MOMENT

most of all.

Everything
you now know
was once
unknown.

LET IN
THE NEW.

AT EVERY MOMENT,

THE WORLD IS WHISPERING OPPORTUNITIES.

Listen closely.

STAY STRONG.

WITH SPECIAL THANKS TO THE ENTIRE COMPENDIUM FAMILY.

CREDITS:

WRITTEN BY: **M.H. CLARK**
DESIGNED BY: **SARAH FORSTER**
EDITED BY: **AMELIA RIEDLER**
CREATIVE DIRECTION BY: **JULIE FLAHIFF**

PHOTOGRAPHY CREDITS:

COVER, PAGE 5: VINTAGE CLOUDBURST BY: **DAVID M SCHRADER / VEER**
PAGE 6: ROUND AND ROUND BY: **GRÄFIN. / PHOTOCASE.COM**
PAGE 9: DANCE ON IN BY: **SARAH FORSTER**
PAGE 10–11: TAHOE WATERS BY: **SARAH FORSTER**
PAGE 15: SCHMETTERLING BY: **JUDIGRAFIE / PHOTOCASE.COM**
PAGE 16: THE TREES ARE MOVING BY: **RAFFIELLA / PHOTOCASE.COM**
PAGE 18–19: SHI SHI SUNSET BY: **SARAH FORSTER**
PAGE 21: FLACHS – IG BY: **JMDPHOTO / PHOTOCASE.COM**
PAGE 25: ABFLUG BY: **PRENZ66 / PHOTOCASE.COM**
PAGE 29: FEMME ROOTING BY: **JESSICA MAY RITA KOHUT**
PAGE 30–31: FEATHER BY: **SARAH FORSTER**
PAGE 34–35: EIFFEL TOWER BY: **SARAH FORSTER**
PAGE 37: NEW YORK CITY BY: **SARAH FORSTER**
PAGE 38–39: GRAND CANYON BY: **SARAH FORSTER**
PAGE 41: ODE TO JOY BY: **JOEL SISEL & SARAH FORSTER**
PAGE 44–45: FUNKENALARM 2 BY: **MCDEEKEY / PHOTOCASE.COM**
PAGE 47: WHEAT FIELD BY: **SIERRA FISH**
PAGE 51: CITY DOUBLE EXPOSURE BY: **BERT.DESIGN / GETTY IMAGES**
PAGE 55: INSIDE THE TUBE BY: **SHANNON STENT / GETTY IMAGES**
PAGE 56: JUMP BY: **PARTICULA / PHOTOCASE.COM**
PAGE 59: SPRING BLOSSOMS BY: **SARAH FORSTER**
PAGE 60: QUAKING ASPEN BY: **JOHN WANG / GETTY IMAGES**
PAGE 64: FIGHT ON BY: **SARAH FORSTER**

ISBN: 978-1-935414-83-4